AF247578

The Darkness in my Pockets

Olga Cabral

GALLIMAUFRY
SAN FRANCISCO
1976

ACKNOWLEDGMENTS

Some of these poems have appeared in the following publications: *GALLIMAUFRY* ("Literary Awards," "The Meadow," and "House of the Poet"); *THE NEW YORK QUARTERLY* ("Are They Listening?"); *SOUTH AND WEST* ("Orange"); *LIGHT* ("Help!"); *POETRY NOW* ("Lillian's Chair," and "The Stone People"); *BOB ARNOLD'S WORKSHOP* ("Bell in Water"); *N.Y. POETS' COOPERATIVE* ("5 & Dime").

"Occupation: Spinster" originally appeared in *WE BECOME NEW: POEMS BY CONTEMPORARY AMERICAN WOMEN*, edited by Lucille Iverson and Kathryn Ruby, and published by Bantam Books, Inc. It is copyright © 1975 by the author. "Poem About Death" originally appeared in *FOR NERUDA, FOR CHILE*, edited by Walter Lowenfels, and published by Beacon Press.

"The All-Night Laundromat" and "The Arrest" will appear in *POETRY NOW*. "In the Presence of the Bat Gods" will appear in *THIRD RAIL*.

"The Music of Villa-Lobos" is from *TAPE FOUND IN A BOTTLE*, copyright © 1976 by the author.

Library of Congress Cataloging in Publication Number: 76-5585
ISBN Number: 0-916300-03-X

The publication of this volume was made possible in part
by a grant from the National Endowment for the Arts.

Published by *GALLIMAUFRY*
359 Frederick Street
San Francisco, California

THE DARKNESS IN MY POCKETS

(For Lillian Lowenfels)

LILLIAN'S CHAIR

Lillian has just arisen from her chair.
She has gone into her garden to commune with snails
to answer the birds' questions.
She has left her shawl and her cane
and that iron leg brace.
Won't she need her shawl in the garden?
Won't she be feeling the cold?

And she has forgotten her sling
thrown it carelessly aside—
the crumpled black satin
in which she cradled her dead arm
for seventeen years.
In one hand she took her straw basket
in the other her pruning shears:
"That bush needs seeing to," she muttered
and went looking for red clover, queen anne's lace.

What is she doing so long in the garden?
Where has she gone with her red hair?
She just grew tired of sitting and watching.
A vivid light pulled her into the leaves.
Woolen shawl, satin sling, iron brace—
she just walked out on them all.

Left us this empty chair.

LITERARY AWARDS

It is necessary to appear in person
with three copies.

One shall be color-blind.
The second Late Minoan.
The third is optional.

All decisions are irrevocable.
There will be no appeal.

Bring your clavicles
your stone of blueness
the darkness in your shoes and pockets.

In next Thursday's dream
a cash award of old car keys
and a free trip
on the continental drift.

ARE THEY LISTENING?

We are listening. Is anyone speaking?
Who are the speakers? In what tongue do they address us?
What Rosetta Stone will give us the key
to the lost language of the stars?

This blue planet is not timeless.
Nor your eyelashes. Nor the raindrops on your face.
The sun having eaten its hydrogen
will turn cannibal, swallow its own children.

Are they listening? As we are listening?
Will they learn our primitive alphabets?
Is someone writing a poem this minute
on a world that died five million years ago?

Perhaps there are only dead languages
and we are the loneliest accident, and the luckiest.

THE MUSIC OF VILLA-LOBOS

Someone is speaking a lost language.
It is the music of Villa-Lobos.
I try to remember: where was I
born? And from what continent
untimely torn? I might have been
a priestess among the caymans
guarding the eye-jewel of the
crocodile god. I might have sailed
orinocos of diamonds, seas of coconuts
leased the equator for life and learned
my ancestral language.

But I have only some old sleeves of rain
in a trunk with spiders
to remember my ancestors by.
They have left me
nothing, and I have forgotten
that island of my birth
where the sun in his suit of mirrors
was seen once only with my vast fetal eye.

But in the music of Villa-Lobos
a god with a tower of green faces
comes striding across cities
of permafrost, and I am summoned
once again to the jaguar gardens
guarded by waterfalls
where the hummingbird people are at play
far from the cold auroras of the north.

OCCUPATION: SPINSTER

Lawyer Dickinson's spinsterly daughter
was mad the neighbors said: she
hid inside a snowflake
there being nowhere else to go.
Fallen lightyears
from fields of star-hooved Taurus
into puritan body/sapphic brain
she the lost Pleiad
mourned for the company of her blinding Sisters.

> (They come before us, the Victorian women
> prisoners of muslin caged in taffeta
> with their dim hair and drowning eyes:
> women of genius warm and womanly
> who burned in that dry spare air to their
> crystal bones.)

In Amherst Emily lived on
though the world forgot
moving with calm coiled hair through tidy days.
Her face shrank to a locket. She explored
miniaturized worlds known only to moths and angels
walked to the far side of a raindrop—
trespassed
on Infinity.

> (How many Emilies
> coughed and stitched
> died too young in furnished attics
> while the Universe boiled over in its
> starry Pail?)

AN ANCIENT ALPHABET
(For Aaron)

Because you were writing your poems backward
an ancient alphabet
from right to left as in mirrors
because the letters resembled doorways
of cedar beams
letters like pillars
in rows like walls or palisades
because they rose like cities on the page
because they danced in black gabardine
because they were the strong black birds of prophecy
that flew out of the fires of immolation
because I saw these letters resembled commandments
commandments to live
because they stormed across the page
an ancient alphabet
like brotherly armies with linked arms
I knew your poems were strong and beautiful
I knew they were invincible
because you were writing your poems backward
I loved you then and forever
for one and twenty years

ORANGE

At the top of the city I
sit at my rickety table
ready for my breakfast orange.
I glance at the weather below—
rough out there today!
My little room rocks
like a boat. 40 million windows
have disappeared under fog
and boiling gases. And I'm to sail
those sunken reefs.

But I would rather look at my orange
for another hour if I could
and rub my face against its
textured skin
whose pores exude such a wild perfume
like a thousand alhambras in moonlight
and I would rather contemplate
the dazzle of its corona
on the plastic tablecloth which is blue as the
                mediterranean—
a miniature breakfast
côte d' azur
at the top of smoke-bound gray
Manhattan.

And today I wish I were
the color of an orange—
I would give a fiesta for myself!
And I wish my pores could sweat
perfumed oil of tropical groves.
Orange, naranja, the sun
isn't stopping off here today.
Look up, people! Look up,
you 40 million deadeyed windows—
it's my orange shining
through the fog!

POEM OF WEDNESDAY

Somehow or other
I'm stuck in Wednesday
and can't get out.
You say it isn't bad
this Wednesday? Well, consider
if you've nowhere to go
but Wednesday
if the borders have been sealed
and your passport to the next
24 hours
has been lifted.

I am looking for Thursday
on Wednesday
Thursday a way out
to Friday.
But I'm still here in Wednesday
a country of dolts and smugglers
Wednesday's cares the color of
gray phlegm.

Wednesday when the week sags
like a wet washline
Wednesday with its clocks
always turned to the walls
Wednesday when the bus arrives
to get you out of there
but passes you by
the Chief Smuggler waving from the driver's seat
leaving you at the curb
stranded
in the middle of Wednesday.

Wednesday with its sullen hotels
and rundown cafés
always full
no reservations
waiters pushing you out
mumbling:
      Oversubscribed.
           Oversubscribed.
                Oversubscribed.

Wednesday when nobody has met you
and you have met nobody
but clerks and smugglers
all day
and Friday
Friday with its metallic
blue butterflies
a far-off country
across sealed borders
of perilous time zones.

5 & DIME

They were visitors to penny arcadias.
They were people lost in subways.
They were the poor seeking Layaway Plans.
They were trapped in the hanging gardens
of the giant 5 & Dime.

They were smelling the plastic flowers.
They were reveling in mothproof forests.
They were dazzled by bloodless blossoms:
Kodachrome fuchsias, whiter-than-whites,
deadly reds, cryogenic blues.

There were angels guarding the exits
in frightwigs. Bibles grew wild
and abundant as shrunken heads.
In and out of the tropical houseplants
birds flew around in straightjackets.

The Queen of Sheba sold them corncures
when they tired. They sat on the plastic grass.
Picked plastic fruit from the plastic trees
and admired how dewdrops hung motionless
around the clock and season.

Was it heaven? Was it hell? It was wrinkleproof
and guaranteed not to bleed. It wasn't real
but nobody minded. They were prisoners
trapped in the nervous breakdown
of the American Dream.

THE ALL-NIGHT LAUNDROMAT

Sacks full of soiled dreams are brought to the laundromat.
It is open all night. Somnambulists are welcome.
Inside it is cosy. An artificial rain on the windows.
The hum of the machines in their cycles. The Proprietor
                    always absent.

The people open their bundles. They shake out the sheets.
Insomnia falls out. And some grayish fears.
It all goes into the soapsuds and bleach.
The people too become clearer, cleaner.
They pore over each other's socks. They share each other's
                    shirts.
They exchange garments lovingly faded and worn.

Swish-swash. Everything will come out spin-dry and shriven
and will go home in someone else's laundry bag.
Let whoever will wear your disguises, your patches and flags.
The people have gone to sleep in the warm dryers.
There they go round and round chasing their underwear.

Time to wake them. Time to tell them
they can go home. A new cycle begins all over again.

THE ARREST

There I was
right in the middle of
someone else's dream:

Hey, you!
This is trespassing!
He blew a whistle.

This is not real,
I scoffed.
I never dream three-legged men.
And escaped into my own dream.

There he was again:
Hey, you!
This is trespassing!

Get out! I said.
Get out of my dream!

He blew the whistle.
We've got it wired, he said.
Electrodes. We can make you dream
anything we please.

POETS LOST IN SUBWAYS

All these arrows
doubling back on themselves
all those traffic signs
in an incomprehensible language
all those turnstiles
admitting us to armageddon
for a token
all those subway faces
anxious about timetables.

I ask myself each day:
where is the water of pearl
that will split this stone?
Where is the cataract that falls
from the stone's dry heart?
I declare myself innocent
of this. I declare
we are all innocent
of something.

All those coughing overcoats
hugging their wet newspapers
stumbling through metallic fogs
and miasmas of urine—
they are only trying
helplessly hopelessly
to get through the tunnels
from one day
to another day.

Why don't they arrest
those walls of stained dentures?
Serve a summons on those mops
smelling of ammonia and vomit?
Clap handcuffs on those galvanized pails
full of slimy secrets?
Put them all in the lockup
in an unused station on the IRT
where no trains will stop
for a thousand years.

It is no wonder
a new race of giant graffiti
has captured the subways
it is no wonder
names, names in their anger
multiply in darkness
crawl along walls
fall from the ceilings like spiders.

Words agile and hairy
leap over us like acrobats
as we run through mean tunnels
hearing our footsteps like stones tumbling
                    after us.

Names vivid in color
colors of the four directions
the four winds and the fifth wind
push into crowded trains with us
joggle our elbows
blaze themselves on our eyeballs.

Names, names we never met
never were introduced to
dazzle our weak eyes;
eerie syllables we never heard
force us to learn their new alphabets
their musical notations
read their crowded history
on rush hour walls.

Those whose names were given
in disappearing ink
name themselves again
in manifestos against nothingness
those whose names were written
on the heads of rusty nails
sign their names in letters
tall as monuments.

Goya of the *Capricchos*
wearing a Young Lord's purple beret
adds his name in flowing fuchsia
to the living mosaic
the interlocking names
on the walls of breath on the walls
of poets lost in subways.

(HELP!)

i.

Help! I am trapped inside a pair of parentheses!
Will somebody read me the sentence
in which I am imprisoned?
What is the meaning of the paragraph
in which I briefly appear? How did I get stuck
in the quagmire of this terrifying page
that sounds like gibberish?
Does it make any sense at all
with/or without me?
Does the Twentieth Century
make sense at all?

ii.

Help! I'm a prisoner in an index file!
I've been stapled with steel hooks—I'm bleeding
all over the 4 x 5 cards!
A facsimile of myself is masquerading
in my place. I've been reduced to
some holes in a punch card, a code number
in somebody's data bank.
No one has noticed this imposter:
myself who daily impersonates myself.
What was the original like
I wonder?

ENIGMA OF THE SCISSORS GRINDER

The scissors grinder's fingers
are flying into space:
the scissors is grinding him.
He is being filed
thin as a blade.
His ears have a fine
edge. His nose
could cut cheese and butter.
His honed face sharpens
his bones hum and sing
like carbon steel.

The tools that he tended
stand over him now:
all the scissors and knives.
A trim pair of shears
keeps its sharp little foot
on the pedal. The wheel
turns, the gray whetstone
hisses and flies
whirling revolving. And the scissors
grinder is becoming
so sharp so fine
he could cut a feather
with his thin breath.

Getting smaller and ever
smaller he at last
disappears in a stream
of blue sparks: the grinder
ground down to nothing
by his own
grindstone.

ROSE

I walk into the flower
room after vivid room
doors of silk shut behind me
I am the prisoner of the flower
I feel the power of its softness
my feet slide on satin floors
I walk its corridors of minute immensities
there are perfumes here that will change me
there are walls too brilliant to bear
there are carpets woven of nerves
there are velvets more polished than steel
there are caverns that open like eyes
I have never seen such colors
this red is deeper than sleep
there are carmines lakes and alizarins
that have not yet been invented
I think I am the first one here
I think these rooms have been waiting for me
I think I can leave when I want to
I think when I return I will be different
you will not know where I have been

OBJETS PERDUS

Papa Freud the last
Jehovah
presides over the march of parentheses
the gotterdammerung
of teakettles.
An army of ants keeps bringing his *ibids*.
His feet slide into them.
They fit him perfectly.
It happens all the time in the museum of coughs.

STONE

In the stone
>   a forest's footprint.
In the stone
>   an epoch's hieroglyph.
In the stone
>   a mineral creature.
In the stone
>   the earth's heart beats.

A stone:
>   of an ancient race
>   wise and sharp-wrinkled.
A stone:
>   that witnessed leviathan
>   deaths of oceans.
A stone:
>   that was itself a mountain
>   trampled by ice packs.
A stone:
>   that marched to the sea
>   when continents crumbled.

Now the lost mountain returns from sea-burial
to lie in my hand:
a stone.

A stone:
>	with its own cliff faces
>	and deep ravines.
A stone:
>	with a message written
>	from glaciers.
A stone:
>	lying among its brothers
>	at the edge of the ocean.
A stone:
>	that I found and left
>	for the world's necklace.
A stone:
>	that will come to its end
>	and grow smaller and smaller.
A stone:
>	that will forget its history
>	and become sand.

Mountain into
stone
into
sand
into...

Sand
underfoot
thick as
galaxies/

galaxies
overhead
thick as
sand.

BELL IN WATER

There is a bell in the harbor.
Rocking with the tide it
tells the moon if it has clearance
for deepwaters.
All night the currents tug. It speaks
a watery language I
remember only in sleep.
The bell in water draws me
to the shore. I walk
on fossils. I step back in time
enter the house of the shell
and meet
my sea-self.

I am soft.
Snug in my shell-house. The tide
swings me about. I would be happy but
remember
something I must do.
I seek
the turbulence. Am caught
in lashing combers.
The wave lifts me
and breaks me.

I lie on sand
and will myself to be
a foot.
I am all foot now
slime-foot flowing
the first inch on the
billion-year journey
to the harbor
with its night-moored ships and
tolling of
channel bell.
Somewhere
along the darkened shore a
shell lies empty.

THE STONE PEOPLE

(Bryce Canyon)

Looking at the stone people
below us on the canyon floor
the standing stone people
left over from an earlier creation
a mile down from the canyon's rim
where we stood together in the wind and the light:
a convocation of stones
a great crowd in silent assembly
all upright
facing one way

facing toward a rock
of towering light and loneliness
as though they were waiting for it to speak
stone listening to stone
as if after aeons
light would break from its lips
in a longed-for word
a sign
something in the stone crying to be born
something that wants to be alive

Looking at the stone people
on that day pinned to the light
wondering how they had been summoned there
had they traveled far on their stone feet
and why had they arranged themselves like this
rough stones in a rough semicircle
standing through light and weather
darkness runaway stars
and millennia of birds

at that moment of wind and light
we knew
what the naked hunter knew:

earth's creation is never finished
there are many surprises
we are not the sum of it all

THE MEADOW

(Homage to Paul Klee)

i.

To make insects equal among stars
to make a ladder so dogs could sniff at the moon
to make a man jump from the moon with grasshopper legs
to make a bird so blue the sea would fly after it

ii.

This is the meadow where we meet
the place on the circle
where everything crosses
in time
at the bottom of sleep the garden
before eden
here because a poet dreamed it
"everything is comparable to everything"
everyone is becoming everyone
in this garden the ancient sounds
the language all creatures
speak
the glyph of plants
and a yellow bird that can walk upside down on the sky
and a falling-up rain

iii.

If I send my eye walking without hands
it will represent me
if I send my foot that is waiting by the road
it will follow the arrow
the clearly marked arrow
that points to the axis of the universe

iv.

Here alphabets dance
with angels
an angel equals
the astral body of a fly
here nothing is more
and nothing less

v.

Violins have leaped from their skins
left them behind like the debris of cities
and brought nothing with them
but the long
cry of the bow
it is raining whole operas
a little man with a pendulum in his head
walks by humming

vi.

If I were tortured
wired to sun and moon
if I saw my fragments run away
and flee each other
if the birds put on masks
and became strangers
if a chorus of dead geniuses
waggled their beards from among the meteors
causing the dunes to lose their gayest grasses
I would escape
in the ship of a snail
I would turn into a woodlouse
and go away and join
a traveling circus

vii.

For the primordial cell
exists across ages
and even on distant stars
dances in a red shirt

viii.

Little symbols run around
in panic
endearing genes
new creatures new possibilities
crowding each other like passengers
in a railroad station
waiting for the train
all that exist are
"fragments
of reality"
notes
on a musical score

ix.

This is the meadow where we meet
the peaceable kingdom of
creatures
beginning/becoming
themselves and each other
living and loving
under a hatful of sky

TEETH

Andean cities
rocked by terrifying shoulders
flung about like fleas by the earth's angry skin
how many times
the Indian cities tumbled the temples spilled their stairs
through the stone cycles
but the people
rebuilt replanted and divided the crops
as the sun willed.

But there are disasters even worse than earthquakes:
gigantic jaws that came out of the sea
teeth that are gnawing you to pulverescence.

Almighty molars grindstones of God
that grind granite and crumble your purest crystal
teeth that tear at your belly pregnant with minerals
teeth of the universal pawnshop the black-suited Godfather
teeth that subtract and deprive and bereave
teeth that extract like giant forceps
teeth that clutch and clench in the rigor mortis of an extinct
                    century
rapacious teeth ravenous teeth gleaming like bathtubs
teeth of the colonial commercial the gigantic dentures that
                    hang in the air
teeth of the vitreous smile of diplomacy
teeth made of gravestones polished by generals
teeth that gnaw at your continental bone and spit out graves
teeth
that are chewing up the world that have bitten
the earth in two.

ITINERARY FOR AN ABANDONED CITY

When you arrive
you will find the city abandoned.
You will set out alone
on the street of blue doves
and find the small whitewashed hotel.
It will be empty
and have a FOR SALE sign.
You will go inside
your suitcase heavy so heavy
with its paper roses its cloak of butterflies
its unfinished sentences.
You will climb the stairs
and find the room.

It will be the same room
looking as it had always looked.
There will be fresh linen and clean towels
laid out for the expected guest
and you the stranger
will rest awhile from your travels
wondering whom to call.

If you will pick up the telephone
and dial Time
a scolding clock will answer.
If you hang up and decide to call Weather
a banal voice will tell you
the weather has ceased operations
and thank you for calling.

Out in the street you will go strolling
down lonely colonnades
past the talking statues
admiring the monumental slide rule.
Then turning left at the cobblestoned square
you will enter the little street
and remember
this was why you journeyed to the city.

You will come to a house.
Inside the house there is night.

THE VISIT

The storm bird
flying at me
came from a
hole in the north:

"I am Ice Bird.
I will show the way
through the crevasse
of black ice."

I watched
through veils of water
as it balanced
on the wild gusts

and floating
to my window
it fixed me
with its eye.

Looking deep
into the bird-eye
I felt a shock
of recognition

perhaps the eternal
bird-spirit:
felt my arms lift
as I veered

and spiralled upward
in the clean storm:
coldness wildness
matching wing to wing.

My self a heap
of old clothes
left in an
empty room.

MAYAKOVSKY

Mayakovsky has come back to New York.
Has invented himself again.
Look—he is huge
everything big, too big.
He has outgrown poetics at the sleeves.
His wrists hang out.
On the way to the poetry reading
he has slashed his wrists.

Here come the poets of fashion.
They clamber into the creases of his yellow vest
and wait for him to begin.
Chi-ri, chi-ri, say the poets
for once all agreeing.

Look! A gigantic blue eye
of heavy seas, groundswells!
Look! A taiga on his forehead—
a painted aborigine!
Look! His wounded wrists drip red
syllables. His poems run wild in the streets!

Mayakovsky
        Mayakovsky
pure aborigine of poetry
the sun follows you around
a fiery little dog.
A giant foot
not a ballet slipper
shakes St. Marks and the Brooklyn Bridge
and every bronze and marble backside
felt your colossal kick:

I spit
> *on the tons of bronze*
I spit
> *on the slimy marble*

Mayakovsky
    Mayakovsky
even though you are dead the Poetry Police
still can't catch up with you.

IN THE PRESENCE OF THE BAT GODS

(For Victor Jara)

In the Soccer Stadium of my brain
I see you walking your last mile
your guitar held to your body
as you go to the interrogation

       this is your last audience
           Victor
       it is time to ring down the darkness

We do not know who will be next
the firing squads get no rest
everyone is on someone's list
have you signed up for the Soccer Stadium?
Send me your list
I'll send you mine

This is your last audience
      Victor
you come
into the presence of the torturers
lords of the underworld
      the nine hells
           where the jaguar sun disappears
           swallowed
                by the snake of darkness
      under the earth
           at the bottom of everything that exists
      in the presence of ancient bat gods
           covered with death emblems.

Here they come with their white kid gloves and gasmasks
here they come to teach you
        what it means to have
                smart bombs
                modern interrogation techniques
                special forces
                death squads
                        children's coffins
                        shrieks in the night
                        wailing in the *poblaciones*
fat generals tattooed with swastikas
bat gods tattooed with death emblems

Victor Victor
what did they do with your hands?
When they cut off your hands
        did the hands play
        on invisible guitars
                did your fingers strum
                on the floor of the abbatoir?

A guitar has a frail body
it gets in the way of a war machine
with its music
guilty guilty guilty
the artist always guilty
of life
guilty guilty guilty
the light that streams from the fingers
the last poem the last song
at the wall of execution

Victor Victor
        they killed you with machinegun bullets
        it is forbidden to speak your name in Chile

But your hands
        cannot rest
        pluck music from
        death
        from nothingness
your voice in the energy
        circling
        the earth:
                Así
                golpeará
                nuestro
                puno
                nuevamente

They killed you Victor in the sports stadium
they killed you because it was the national sport

Long after you were dead they kept killing you
        and killing you

HOUSE OF THE POET

Things that exist alongside us in their own domain
things of metal or wood bits of paper or string
things that share our universe oddments of pens and paperclips
things that await us in the morning and take leave of us at night
things that fade in our absence and wrap themselves in shawls
                              of dust
things that grow old alongside us
things that outwit and outwait us
things that will surely outlive us
things that are particles of light and that will return to the light
things that burn in salt things that corrode by their own clocks
things whose crystals realign themselves with the poles

chairs that offer us their laps tables that offer their shoulders
bureau drawers that hold the names of all the drowned
cupboards that contain all the old telephone numbers
closets that hold our hats of invisibility
fountains of feathers conch shells that play Beethoven
lamps of water guarding our dreams from policemen
doors that groan in the night because they remember being trees

angels of ships wooden angels figureheads of women
who stood at vanished prows with draperies of storm
violated statues fallen among the dead china
the glass of apocalypse and the lynched candles
all the stricken things the broken objects that mourn and mourn
in the house of the dead poet Pablo Neruda

POEM ABOUT DEATH

I don't want to die so many small deaths.
The death of somnambulists in all-night cafeterias
or clerks following their steel-file coffins to the grave.
The small funerals of varnishes, job interviews.

I don't want to die the life of AT&T.
The brain bland as gelatin in its brainbox,
a small electrode embedded in its gray crevasses
implanting canned laughter, military commands and jokes stale
                    as frenchfries.

Listen! I have lived from Spain to Spain.
I was young in Guernica. I grew old in Santiago.
I tried to stop all the bleeding, to bandage wounds with
                    petitions.
I tried to stop the blind bombing capability with my fists
                    and cries.

And all the while what deaths! What grandiose harvests
                    of corpses!
What chimneys! What soft targets! What magnificent madhouses!
And the death of choices:
death by hunger or death by the firing squad.

There are deaths and deaths.
There is the death of Kennecott Copper climbing 7/8ths to
                    corporate heaven
as someone is pushed from a helicopter somewhere over Chile
for eating meat instead of garbage for the first time in his
                    life.

You say this is not a subject for a poem?
That it is not even a poem?
That I should leave death to the professionals?
That poetry should be above "all that"?

Listen! There is a wind that slices iron.
The dead keep their accounts. The living grow stronger.
I want to die a little each day living the deaths of the people.
Bleeding because I am alive.

Olga Cabral is a New York poet. Of Portuguese descent, she was born ten degrees north of the equator, in the West Indies. When she was nine months old, her parents moved to the Canadian prairie. From the age of ten she has lived in New York, except for several periods on the West Coast.

Her previous books of poetry are *Tape Found in a Bottle* (1971), *The Evaporated Man* (1968) and *Cities and Deserts* (1959). Her poems have appeared in various literary journals and have been published in seventeen anthologies.

Her occupations have included office worker, art gallery owner, and director of a children's art workshop. She is the widow of the American Yiddish poet, Aaron Kurtz.

The Darkness in my Pockets
is published in an edition of 1,000,
26 of which are lettered and signed by the poet.

Cover lithograph, *Shattered Firmament*,
Copyright © 1976 by Leavenworth Jackson.

Typeset in 10 point Palatino
Designed by Mary MacArthur
Printed at the West Coast Print Center

1976